JULIAN JOSEPH ON **JAZZ**

Music is a miracle in this world of sound and jazz — one of its great marvels. It is mystical, colourful, uplifting, energising, soothing, meditative, gentle, powerful and a force which exists in its own universe. Yet jazz is all around us, absorbed into many other genres and cultures across the globe, expressing all manner of things from conservatism to raciness, from coolness to wildness, from intellect to intuition, from everyday life to that of a secret agent's. These and many more connections enrich the world of sound through jazz. Its myriad associations in cinema, advertising, education, sport and the many industries that music accompanies mean jazz is always in the atmosphere.

Lovers of jazz are intrigued by its unique flavour, infectious pulse, groove and how it's created. Who are these people who direct and control this mercurial ocean of ideas bathed in the blues, tethered and untethered to craft this attractive music in and of the moment? Jazz musicians.

Our very existence as human beings works in exactly the same way as the music. Individuals brought together by choice or design influenced by our strengths, weaknesses and abilities, writing the music of our lives as we go.

Jazz musicians are conjurers, inventors, dreamers, scientists, philosophers, explorers, superheroes, magicians and masters in the alchemy of sound as applied to a super-culture that brings balance to human existence with the vibration of the earth in the physical and spiritual universes.

The appetite to understand jazz has amassed a huge library of information, which we can all tap into and benefit from. The veil has been partially lifted with biographies and analyses to aid insight into the music's practice and its practitioners. The numerous harmonic and melodic vocabularies in jazz filter through its uniquely singular rhythm, an infusion of eloquence in the creation of beautiful music. In this book, I have attempted to get into the philosophy of the jazz sound, with one major directive. The answers are in the music, so keep it simple and embrace listening to the masters of the music. Use your initiative to decipher what the music and its greatest practitioners are trying to tell you. Enjoy this journey, trust yourself, bathe in your own instinct, intelligence and initiative, and connect to your inner jazz musician.

CONTENTS

JAZZ IS A MUSIC OF INITIATIVE

One of the reasons I say that jazz is a music of initiative is because it's like thinking about your life and what you want to fill it with. If you have a certain task at hand, it's better if you figure out how to solve that task yourself rather than asking somebody else.

Musically, if you want to play a blues or improvise, think about what you want to play and how you want it to sound. In considering these things, you are already moving with purpose toward your goal. As you play, experiment and enjoy the music, your action will inform the journey you've already set yourself on. That's your initiative, which will grow as your listening increases and expands into all the steps you take.

01. LISTENING

Begin by listening to as much music as you can. You will find that it seeps into your consciousness and, most importantly, influences how you hear. In a similar way, our accents are formed by what voices we hear around us. Usually we are influenced by our parents at first, then by the people and environments that we hang out in.

Music is exactly the same. The way you start to express yourself verbally is an influence and an amalgam of all those things that have influenced you.

Listening is the most important thing to start with, because without listening you won't know what it is you want to deliver.

YOU CAN LEARN TO LISTEN.

LEARNING TO LISTEN

Listening can be a superficial thing; the music might just be playing in the background and you might not take a single thing in. Sometimes it's not even about taking something in, but listening often enough that you start to recognise things. You will start to look for those things, and then if those things aren't there you'll find yourself asking — where are those things?

After this, you'll engage your critical listening. It becomes about familiarity and about being more directed in how you listen, as there are several ways you can do this. One way is just letting the music wash over you — listening loads of times until something seeps in, until something starts to grab hold. Pop songs are built to grab you on the first listen, and then when you hear it again you recognise it… and they've got you.

FORM

IT'S IMPORTANT TO
UNDERSTAND THAT
THERE IS A FORM.

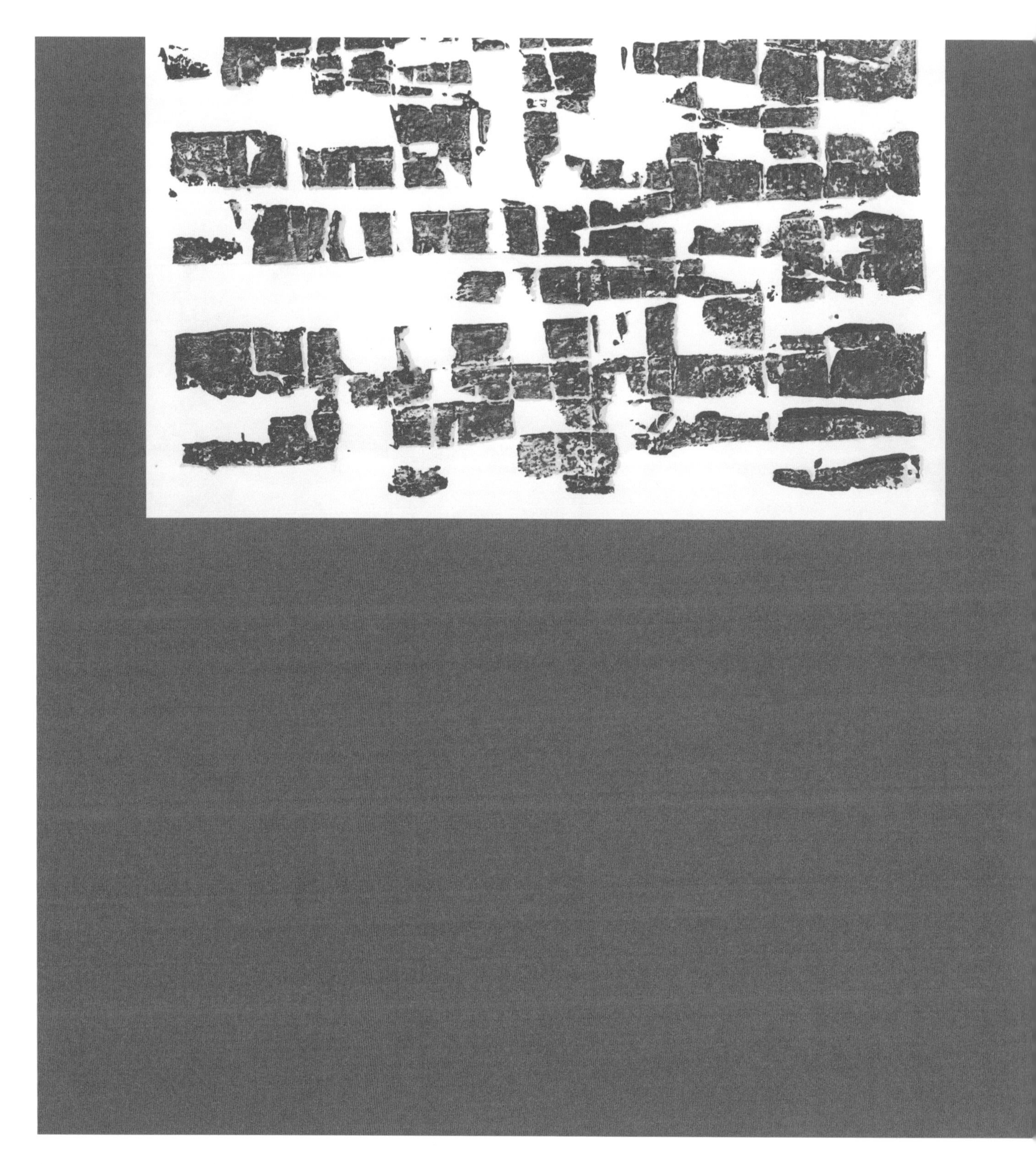

There are two ways to look at this.

When Herbie Hancock first started listening to jazz and trying to learn solos from the recordings of the masters, he didn't realise that the form was repeating. When you hear him improvise it sounds like that spirit revealed a higher truth. Although he fully understands form, he doesn't sound like he's restricted by where the end of it comes. Instead of thinking "okay, I can just repeat to the top again" (and strictly speaking, he does), the music just keeps going, moving forward without boundaries. That's a beautiful way of playing, a great approach to form and it always sounds inspired.

How do you start listening to form? I think one of first things to try and identify is the twelve-bar blues; listening out for the 'one chord', the 'four chord' and the 'five chord'. See how they operate. Try to hear how harmonies repeat, or how the bass line is moving. That's your first way to identify what's going on. You can do that on every tune and I think if you get used to doing it within the blues, and feeling where the changes happen in a blues, it makes you more receptive to doing it on other tunes.

DEVELOPING A RELATIONSHIP WITH THE MUSIC

There are lots of technical aspects in music that you don't need to know.

What you do need to know are the ways to develop a relationship with the music. How? How do you develop a relationship with the music? Through familiarity and interest. This is how we develop a relationship with anything. We listen to our favourite tracks over and over again and we start to recognise signature sounds.

It might be Louis Armstrong, Charlie Parker — it could be anybody. You listen to that one track until you know it, and then listen to another one until you know that. Your ear follows it — I call this your "ear tracking the music". You'll find yourself singing along with Louis Armstrong, with Charlie Parker. This is how you develop your relationship with the music.

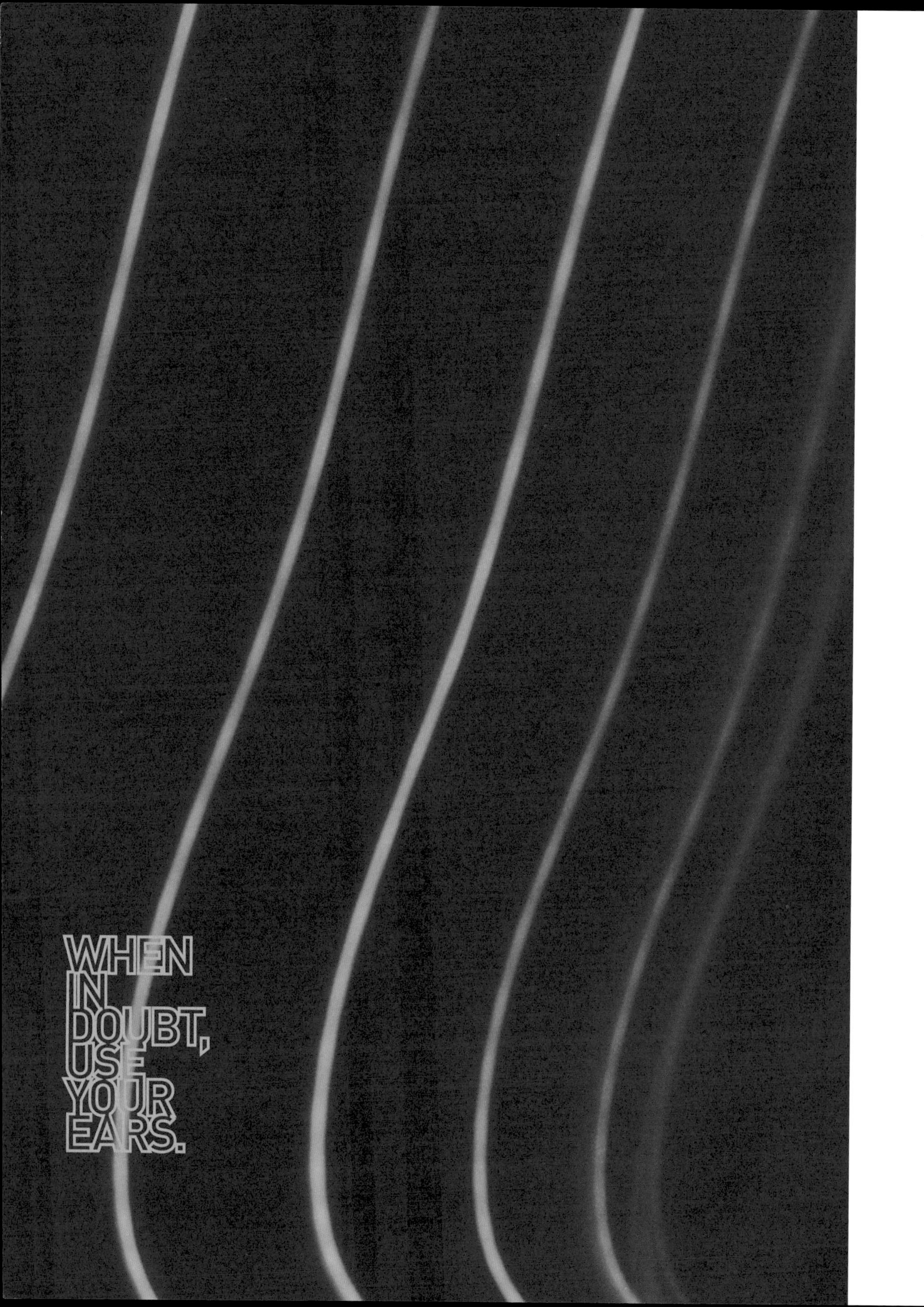
WHEN
IN
DOUBT,
USE
YOUR
EARS.

SINGING ALONG

When in doubt, use your ears.

You don't only have to listen out for your own instrument; try listening to others and singing or tapping along. Some people listen and all they can make out is a big jumble — nothing particularly goes in. Listen in portions. Just focus on one thing at a time.

It really helps to guess what's coming up. Try to sing along with the solo. You can learn note-by-note, stop it and repeat, and repeat again. When you come to a bit that's particularly difficult, you can just isolate it. You can do this four bars at a time, one phrase at a time, or even less. The more you do it, the more the whole thing will come together in your mind.

Keep doing this and you'll suddenly find you have this huge panoramic view: you can see the whole sound. You're using your ears to see, and that's the way to get into music.

one of the greatest gifts of music is sharing it.

LISTENING WITH OTHERS

Your friend might tell you to check out a tune, and you will — perhaps because you like them or respect their taste or ability in music. Even if you don't immediately like it, you'll put the time into listening to it. It's also great to listen with others. Everyone hears music differently and you'll come to realise that other opinions help to shape your own.

02.

THINKING ABOUT JAZZ

For The Newcomer

Jazz invites people to share.

You can participate just by listening and watching, in the same way you might gain from playing for others. When the music is really engaging it becomes conversational. You can see how the bass player is playing with the drummer and how the drummer is playing with the piano player, and how they're sharing the feeling of the music and bringing it together cohesively. This sense of sharing is an innate part of jazz.

It has the wrong reputation because people find it inaccessible. People think that because everybody's playing at the same time it's a cacophony, which doesn't make any sense. But it does make sense.

Jazz is best when you're in the room checking it out. It's great on record, but it's even better live. It's about human experience and connection. For the newcomer, approaching the music as a listener, you can just be there and enjoy it. Take it in. If you don't get it straight away, just enjoy the people who are enjoying it around you, until you start to enjoy it. It will come.

The same goes for the player. The wonderful thing about the music is that you can engage and play, no matter what level you're at. How many times do we see young kids playing with more experienced professionals? They may have just about learned to play through a blues form, or learned two chords. With those two chords the professionals will ask

What are those two chords?

What tempo would you like to play at?

Even with these limited parameters, they can all make music together. The elation of the newcomer playing with somebody who's great, with a whole band of people who are really experienced — you can't beat that. And you don't get that in any other type of music, where an absolute beginner can play with the top guys. The music thrives on sharing the moment.

What is jazz?

Music is defined by its greatest players, its most celebrated players and its most celebrated artists. If you're ever confused about what jazz is, just check it out by listening to one of the greats. It's as simple as that.

One of the most frequently-asked questions is 'what is jazz?' That's because everybody's confused about what it is — is it just anything? If it's got a bit of improvisation in then is it jazz? No. Jazz is a specific thing. It's got to have swing in it — its binding rhythmic impetus and continuum. It's got to have the blues — its sound and cultural signature of optimism. There are elements of the music that don't typically represent this as the flavour can be disguised, but the real source of jazz comes from swing and blues.

You've got to know what that is if you're going to be talking about any part of your music being jazz. Jazz is not some namby-pamby music — it is strong, visceral, inviting, expressive, broad, sad and joyful. It's got everything in it.

It's the manifestation of the human in music.

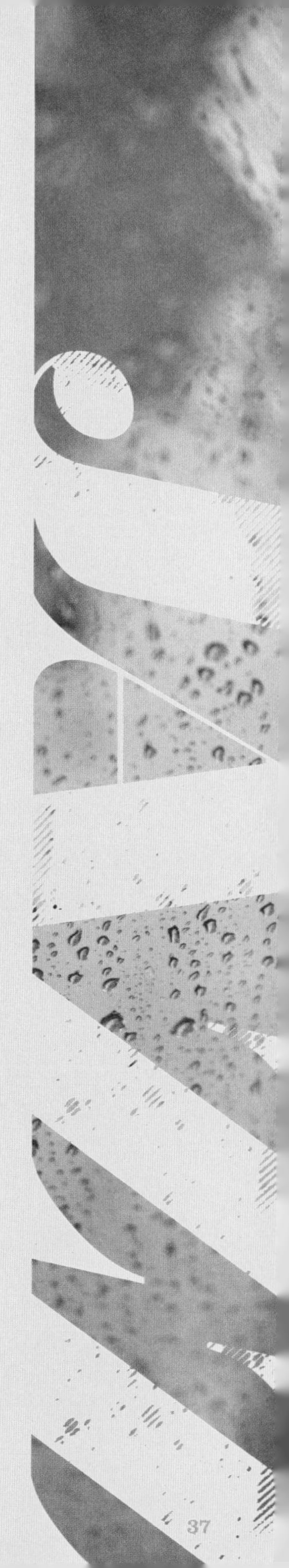

WHAT IS

COMPOSITION

I think one of the things I should say is that my ability to learn in jazz is fuelled by constantly writing. I compose all the time. Often when I was a child, when I would start to learn a tune or a standard, I would just make it into an original composition. It's just my natural way.

I come from a concept of timelessness; I don't believe that what's contemporary is the only thing that has value. What's popular on the radio, who the new guy is, or the new girl, or the new whomever. I don't come from that concept. I come from the concept where everything exists all in the same time.

When I was a child I used to just roll the dial on the radio and just listen. If something sounded interesting, I'd tune in and listen to that because I was inquisitive. I just wanted to hear something. We would listen to Russian folk music, or Bulgarian dance music, or we'd listen to some funk and R&B, or some Bob Marley or some reggae.

So, if I'm listening to Baroque music, that's just as valid as listening to Wayne Shorter; my search for music is broad and wide. With online streaming platforms and the incredible access that we now have to music, you can just find things. All of this music becomes part your musical identity and becomes absorbed.

SE1 ⊖ London Bridge/Borough
020 7407 2690. www.themiller.co.uk

JOSH ROUSE

American alt-country and alt-pop singer-songwriter. Tonight, 7pm. £20.
Union Chapel, Compton Terrace, N1
⊖ Highbury & Islington

Vaudeville 2.30pm mats Thu & Sat

Edith Piaf

THE SONGS OF SCOTT WALKER

Elena, Pam, Angie & Sam, Archie, Otto, Michael Henry

Scott Walker's music performed by a band including Gavin Friday, Jarvis Cocker, Nigel Rie..., Dot Allison, Damon Albarn. Tonight-Sat, 7.45pm.

Barbican Theatre, Silk Street, EC2 ⊖ Barbican 0845 120 7550. www.barbican.org.uk

Ghost Town, Emma & Nick, New London Theatre, Covent Garden, Strand, WC2

TILTING AND BLOODY AWFUL POETRY

MADAME JO JO'S

SCOTT WALKER

Union Chapel, Compton Terrace, N1
⊖ Highbury & Islington
020 7226 1686.
www.unionchapel.org.uk

THE SCRIPT

The soulful Dublin Celtic-rock trio.
Tonight, 7pm. £15, phone for availability

⊖ Tottenham Court Rd 020 72873726.
www.ghetto-london.co.uk

CHEAP$KATES AT MOONLIGHTING

Nu-school disco, old-school hip hop and more. Tonight, 9pm-3.30am. £4-£6.
Moonlighting, 16-17, Greek Street, W1
⊖ Tottenham Court Rd 020 7734 6308.

more. Tonight, 9pm-3.30am. £4-£6.
Moonlighting, 16-17, Greek Street, W1
⊖ Tottenham Court Rd 020 7734 6308.
www.moonlightingnightclub.co.uk

DEATHDISCO AT NOTTING HILL ARTS CLUB

Rock'n'roll, indie and punk, plus live bands

ends Jan 24. £17.50-£47.50.
**Gielgud Theatre,
33, Shaftesbury Avenue, W1**
⊖ Piccadilly Circus
0844 482 5130.
www.delfontmackintosh.co.uk

0844 482 5130
www.delfontmackintosh.co.u

THE COMEDY STORE PL

Improvised comedy from Paul M
Simpson, Colin Sell, Andre Vincer
Webster. Tonight, 8pm. £15.
Comedy Store, 1a, Oxendon S

I like to listen to everything, but it can be quite specific — sometimes I'll hear an aspect of my playing that I'm trying to work on and then I'll focus on a player and absorb their music.

Sometimes I'll only listen to Duke Ellington or Prokofiev, for months on end. My ear doesn't tire of it. So, my listening is broad. Sometimes I'll listen to some Shirley MacLaine just because I want to remember those times and I need to hear the fragility in the way she expresses a song. That's because it's something I can relate to when I'm expressing myself on a tune, either written by me or by somebody else.

THE GREAT ABSORBER

Jazz is the great absorber

I always think of jazz as the human being.

The human being can be whatever it wants to be. There are certain things that we lean to naturally, but we hear something, we receive something, we ingest something, and it represents itself through us. The music exists in that same way. In jazz you can take in something from the classical side or something from folk music, but it will become absorbed, used and re-expressed in a jazz way.

ROOTS

Imagine yourself as a leaf.

You are surrounded by other leaves, all part of the same magnificent tree. Most people are only aware of the other leaves around them and don't even consider the tree they're from. It's important to look back and understand where things come from: the seed, the life-giving force, the spirit.

This is the way we are influenced as musicians and listeners. We can look back at the tree and understand the roots of the music we relate to. Looking back is looking forward.

One day you might become a branch, with many of your own leaves. Or maybe you'll become a whole tree.

TYPES OF PLAYERS

In jazz you have every type of player.

There are those who are quite scientific and cerebral, who play lots of patterned gestures — they've really worked out their way of playing. There are those who just seem to imbue this natural sense of understanding — an earthy feeling. There are also those who are more traditional, those who have an encyclopedic knowledge, those who are happy to just be a leaf... All sorts.

Community in jazz is the same as community in civilisation; you can have a mixture of all of these. This is the human landscape.

FREEDOM AND PARALLELS IN HUMANITY

As human beings we want to be free. We want to live a life that's creative, unencumbered, but informed, and we want to reap all the riches from it. It's the same in music. You want to have the sound of all that is great, and know that you can go anywhere and choose to either follow the path laid down by tradition or completely divorce yourself from it and go elsewhere. These are the choices that we make as creative jazz players.

Parallels to this exist in every aspect of human life: the culture, the family and the way that every musician is connected to everybody else. Certain people provide the community that makes it possible for others to play the way they do. The choice of your band is like a choosing your family. I always call music 'the other blood' because once you're connected through music, the bond is never severed.

FINDING YOUR OPINION

I think most of us form opinions from things that we feel we know. So when you have a relationship with an artist or certain subject matter, and you feel you have knowledge there, you form an opinion. Your opinion is usually formed through your own investigation; if you find yourself ill-informed then you need to reach out for more knowledge. If you converse with people who know the music you'll attain that knowledge quite quickly.

Let's look at the whole concept of 'opinion'. Now, if I'm talking to somebody who's only listened to, I don't know, 25 records, pretty much of the same thing, all in one particular niche area within a genre and I've listened to 1,000 records, hundreds in the genre they're talking about and hundreds of others in many other genres, then the weight of my opinion becomes far greater than the person that I'm talking to. This is what we should consider when we're having a conversation with people about music, especially when we're discussing something that somebody feels really familiar with. You have to put their knowledge and their information into perspective — then you can tackle that.

03.

PLAYING JAZZ

you're only a
semitone away
from the right note.

PLAYING ALONG

It's important to set the right environment when you're playing along with a track.

Find something to listen on. Headphones or speakers — whatever works for you. Have your instrument around. Then just start playing along. Make mistakes and get used to the sound around you, and try to find something that fits. If something sounds wrong, then trust your instinct and keep trying until you find something that sounds right.

Not sure how to find the right notes? Go up the chromatic scale until you find one that fits. As we always say in jazz, and indeed in all music, you're only a semitone away from the right note.

If you struggle to memorise, then it means you're not giving yourself enough time. You need to be patient with yourself. How do you memorise using repetition? How do you repeat things without driving yourself insane? Well, drive yourself insane!

You should give yourself the time to memorise.

repeat, repeat, repeat

Give yourself a break.

repeat, repeat, repeat

Give yourself a break.

repeat, repeat, repeat

If you do this several times a day for a few weeks, you'll get it. It's about giving yourself enough time. If you don't get it in two weeks, then get it in three weeks. If you don't get it in three weeks, get it in four — just be patient.

Understand that it will come. It's like learning anything; play it slowly. You might be tempted to play it fast, but if it's full of mistakes then you will practise in the mistakes. You might be playing it fast, but it will sound horrible. Take your time. Figure out the rhythm of your learning and go with that.

memorisation

First start with the melody, then try to develop it in a way which sounds good to you. Keep it simple, then you can spice it up, add chords and get into the more interesting stuff.

Get to know the shape of the piece. Listen to the recording and see how it evolves. Appreciate where it starts and where it goes. Treat it like a story — get to know the narrative until you can become the story-teller.

Once you've memorised a piece, try learning it in a different key. You'll find yourself really getting to know how the chords fit together. You might even stumble across some new ideas; every key has its own character.

Many jazz manuals will tell you to play everything in every key, but you don't necessarily have to do this. Do what feels right to you and keep experimenting until you find what works best for you.

BOOKS

A book can't help you do anything... well, by itself.

This might sound strange to read, but a book is merely a guide to help you experience something. A book will say:

PUT YOUR HANDS ON THE KEYBOARD AND JUST PLAY

There is no room to question:

Do I have to play these notes, or those notes?

You have to use your initiative. The book opens a door but you have to take the initiative to walk through it.

There are many ways to interpret what you find in a book. Some things are going to be literal but most things aren't.

We can all read Shakespeare and see something different in it. You might discuss a story with a friend and they'll have seen something completely different in it. Ideas just start flooding into our minds. They might be different, but no idea is actually 'wrong' — who's to tell you what's right or wrong? You have to trust yourself. If something doesn't make sense, make it make sense for you.

THEORY

For me, all the theory is in the ear.

Yes, you will go to music class and you'll learn what a major scale is, what a minor scale is, what a dominant seventh is... a minor seventh... a flat five... it goes on and on, and it can get very complicated. I think the first thing you have to identify is how the harmony is moving in terms of the bass line. This is something that I concentrate on in my Jazz Five, which I'll mention a bit later.

Find a tune. Listen to the bass line and try to sing along. Try to find out what the bass note is. Sometimes this is the lowest note you can hear, but sometimes the chord is inverted. You might not know which is which immediately, but at least you're thinking in that way.

Cmaj7

E°7

E♭7

E°7

B°7

Cmaj7

Cmaj7

E♭7

It's important to know the difference between major chords and minor chords. Most chords are basically either major or minor and there aren't many more than these. Go back to your favourite tune and try listening out for the harmony. Sing out the notes of chords, starting with the bass note.

Next you can start listening out for diminished and augmented chords, and then looking at extensions — sixths, sevenths, thirteenths, whatever. You can also try to sing the scales that you hear and these are generally chords with a few notes in between. That's about as much theory as you're going to need — to get started!

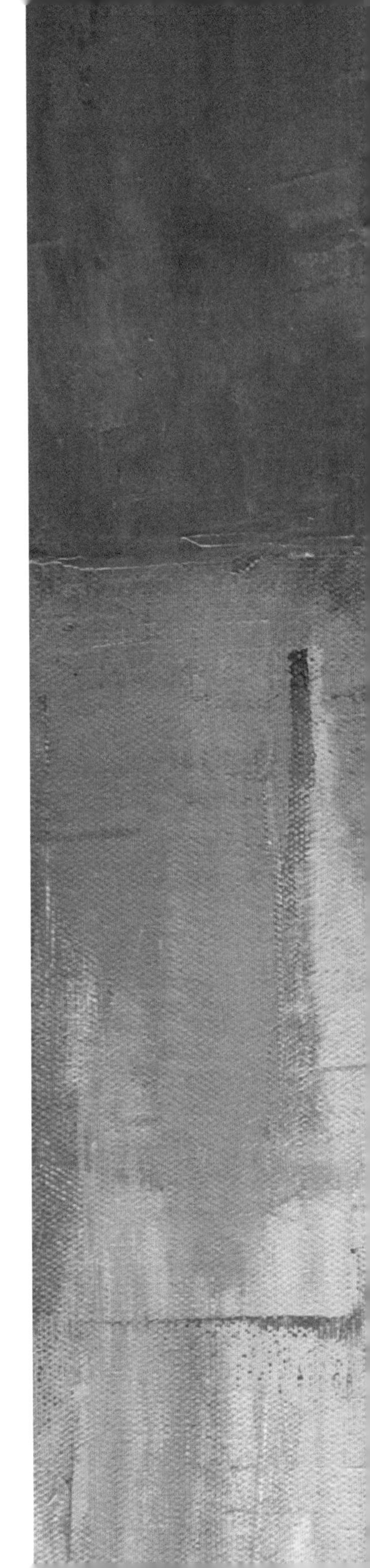

Consolations
No. 6
Db7#9
CΔ7
A
DΔ7
EbΔ7
G-7
AbΔ7
Ab-7
Gb-7
AΔ7#11
D-6
2. Ab-7
B
B-7
Db-7
D-7
E-7
C
DΔ
CΔ7
B-7
Bb7#11
Ab7sus
D
D-
G7
GbΔ7
F7sus
Eb7

WHY DO WE NEED THEORY ANYWAY?

We have to use theory because, as jazz musicians, we're inquisitive. We wonder about what scale we can use, or what chord, or what voicing... It's about collecting your favourite things and building your vocabulary.

That's why we listen to people and say:

I love what Herbie Hancock's doing there. I want that. I want to see that and I want to use that.

or

I want to use that and I don't even know where to put that. But I want it anyway.

You can get away with knowing just the basics, but I always recommend doing some further study — taking a few lessons or theory examinations. This will give you a good grounding as things get more complex.

DESIRE FOR INFORMATION

One great joy of jazz is about the desire — almost greed — for information and for new sounds.

We are constantly surrounded by musical treasures. The best way you can unearth these is to engage and learn. Until you do this, you might not even be aware of the riches of the great players out there.

You'll hear what you like and you'll want to do the same in your own music. You might want to have the technique of Chick Corea with the soulfulness of Horace Silver and the swing of Erroll Garner, mixed up with the intelligence of Bud Powell.

It's like a sweet shop — you'll want to have it all. Initially, this is how you'll forge your identity. You'll start composing, wanting to write a tune just like Herbie Hancock's 'The Sorcerer', because that's the sound you want. So, you grab it. You might really like Chick Corea's 'Windows', so you'll grab some of that.

When you're admiring and learning from your favourites, you almost won't realise that you're taking from the exact source. But what is it that you really want to know? What you really want to understand is: how did Chick become Chick? Then what you might do is look at who Chick was influenced by: Horace Silver, Bill Evans, Bud Powell, Thelonious Monk, Debussy, Bartók and Ravel. Then you might listen to his peers: Herbie Hancock, McCoy Tyner and Keith Jarrett.

Once you start piecing the puzzle together, you can start to understand what makes Chick tick. When you start to get to know Chick, you'll know him even without playing a note that he plays. That's the intelligence that comes with the pursuit of being a jazz musician.

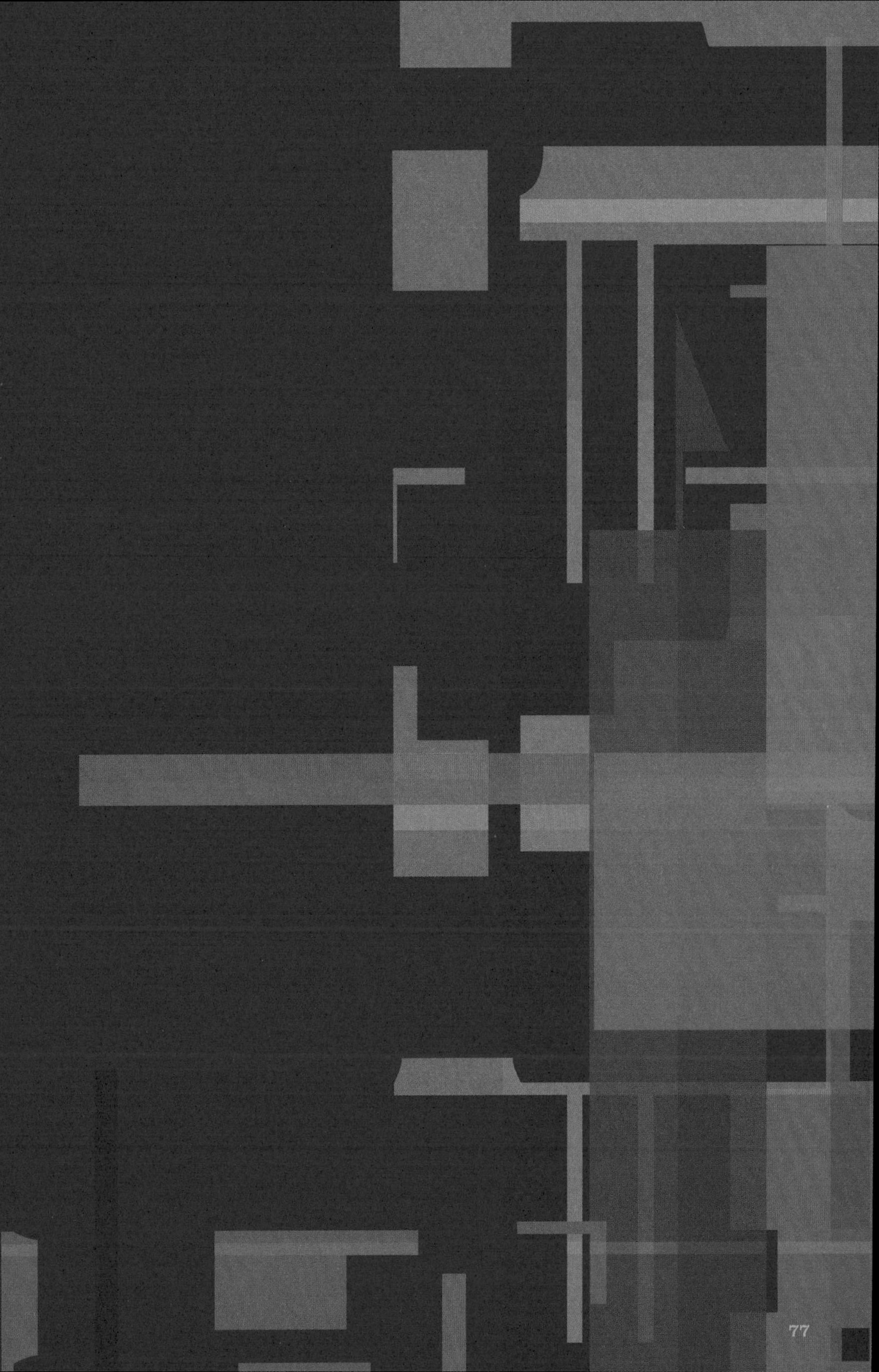

Learning Solos

THE BENEFITS OF LEARNING SOLOS

We all have our favourite artists — singers, writers, musicians. How can we sound more like them? One great way is to learn their solos.

If you're listening with initiative, you're cataloguing in your mind things that you like to hear. You're picking out aspects that speak to you and absorbing them into your spirit. It's important to get into the mindset of identifying and learning what you like. It's not as arbitrary as "I'll sound like them and then not have my own style"; it has taken thousands of hours for your favourite artist to get to that point, and in learning their solos you're engrossing your brain with their wisdom. You might not even know exactly what you want, but you'll never know until you play it.

After a while, you'll have expanded your musical vocabulary to the point where you can say "I want to play that phrase", and it comes out naturally, as an idea. When you get really good at learning solos then you can think "I want that in my targeted vocabulary, and I'm going to put that in every key because I want people to hear that in my playing, no matter what key it's in."

These are some of the benefits of learning solos.

LEARNING SOLOS: LISTENING AND PLAYING

It always starts with listening. Find the recording that you like and just listen to it. Understand the melody, the chords, the structure, the vibe.

Next, have your instrument to hand. Just try playing along. Pick out a few notes here and there; stop it, start it again, try it again. You're looking at it under a microscope. It may take a while at first, but you're training your instinct to be sharper. Learning solos will speed up your ear and your mind. When you listen to the next solo — or another recording of that same track by the same artist, or even another track altogether — you'll start to identify their signature phrases, and you'll be able to more instinctively emulate and play their solos.

The more you do this, the more the ideas go into your brain and your consciousness. But this isn't the only way of learning solos...

TRANSCRIBING SOLOS

A lot can be gained from notating solos from recordings. When you sit, listen and think, you're allowing yourself the time to really consider the music. You can map out the form and structure, the chords, the harmonies, and by transcribing solos you can appreciate the rhythms, tensions and overall shape of the melody. Again, it's like looking at the music and the musician under a microscope. You will improve your understanding and overall familiarity with those specific elements of the solo, and the action of writing out the notes will engrain them in your mind.

So how can you do this? Of course it's best to start with a solid understanding of music notation and music theory — at least enough of a written vocabulary to make sense of pitch and rhythm.

First, try to figure out the pulse and then the metre. Is it in 4? Is it in 3? Is this a jazz waltz, or a slow ballad? Listen out for the bass motion and the other rhythm instruments.

Next, identify the tonality and (if you can) the key. Without perfect pitch you might need an instrument to hand. You'll want to think of the pitches in relation to the tonal centre of the piece and also in terms of its position in the harmony or chord. Doing both will help you to more quickly identify the pitches.

Now you can take down the dots. Work through the recording in portions — even one note at a time, if you have to — and do as much as you can. Take your time and work it out. You'll get better with practice.

In jazz, the term 'transcribing' also means to learn to play a solo without having to write it down. The wisdom is that you encourage your ear and memory to hold the music — and it is highly recommended too!

MOOD AND EMOTION

Of course, your mood and emotional state of mind influence how you play. I don't think you have a choice. It will inevitably come through, but your in-built musical knowledge helps you filter it positively. The more you learn, the more control you have in terms of how you express yourself; you can channel the emotion. If you don't have that control and you're feeling really awful, it can affect your playing and make you sound terrible.

Bud Powell's state of mind was affected by being physically beaten. I think that with anyone who's been brutalised, the scarring comes through in your personal behaviour. It can't help but come through in the way you play musically. There are people who have been hugely scarred by life and it's had an adverse effect on their playing. I think if we look at Bud when he was healthy, he could filter such a wide gamut of emotions: positive, fast and happy, slow and melancholy... he could channel so many things. He's a true artist and we mention him frequently throughout the history of jazz because of the power of his craft. I find it disturbing to see the aftershock of the violence inflicted on him and what did to him as a person and a player. But his artistry was such that, in spite of it all, he expressed beautiful truth in those later years.

Talking more generally for the student, the honesty of how you're feeling and whatever it is you're trying to convey adds to the power of your performance. So, if you're in a particularly melancholy mood, when you're playing the blues you can communicate that melancholy. Or if you're playing a ballad, that melancholy seems all the more poignant. If you're playing an up-tempo piece it could make it a little more introspective; that is actually musically very interesting. So, mood can definitely affect your playing, but it's not a bad thing in the end. It's a good thing.

WHERE WE COME FROM

We should look back on music to know where we've come from. It helps us know where we're going.

You can look at it like this: there is a tree, and there are branches on a tree, and you can take your influence from the corner of a branch. But wouldn't you like to know what the heart of the tree is? Wouldn't you like to come from the tree and be one of the branches? Wouldn't you even like to be a tree?

BUILDING YOUR REPERTOIRE

For the early part of my life, I was not really focused on learning traditional repertoire; I was creating it myself. I was creating it as a consequence of loving the music. I'd hear 'Maiden Voyage' by Herbie Hancock and I'd make up my own version of it, dealing with the rhythm, dealing with the feeling and dealing with the improvisation. This is the beauty of music: you can create your own vocabulary from what you love.

Look for the essence — the simplicity of 'Maiden Voyage', the light latin groove of 'The Girl from Ipanema' or the many diverse takes on 'My Favorite Things' over the years. Learn the melody and the harmony, and then try to learn some of the solos. Find the essence of the tune and use it as a springboard for your own ideas. The more you go through different tunes, the more you'll build a catalogue of things that you can play. You'll find connections as you develop and grow as a musician, but I think the young player has to start from the basics.

THE STORY

The story is in the music.

When you listen, you develop your taste — who and what you like — and you'll start emulating parts of this in yourself. We all emulate people that we admire; we start dressing like them, acting like them, using their vocabulary. We take on little idiosyncrasies of the people we admire. It's human nature and we do that in music... until all of a sudden we don't need to do that. We've grown up. We've gone past that stage and we start to deal with who we really want to be.

Once you've engaged with other people's stories, you can make them part of your own. This is how you develop your narrative as a musician.

Swing is a feeling — it's an approach, intent, expression and result in jazz. When everything flows, connects, pulsates and radiates together with joy, it is said to be swingin'. It's the embodiment of what it means to be human in music. Ascribed specifically for jazz, musics underpinned by the rhythmic pulse descended from the African diaspora share this feeling. It's the times of the past, present and future conjured in the moment — something truly universal.

Like understanding anything in music, use your ears first. Listen to people who swing: check out some tunes by Duke Ellington, Count Basie and Louis Armstrong. Once you lock down the concept of swing, you'll start noticing when people aren't swingin'. That's when you've understood swingin', because most people don't notice it. It's an infectious language and fundamental to the music; you'll find it seeps into your soul and, before you know it, you'll be swingin'.

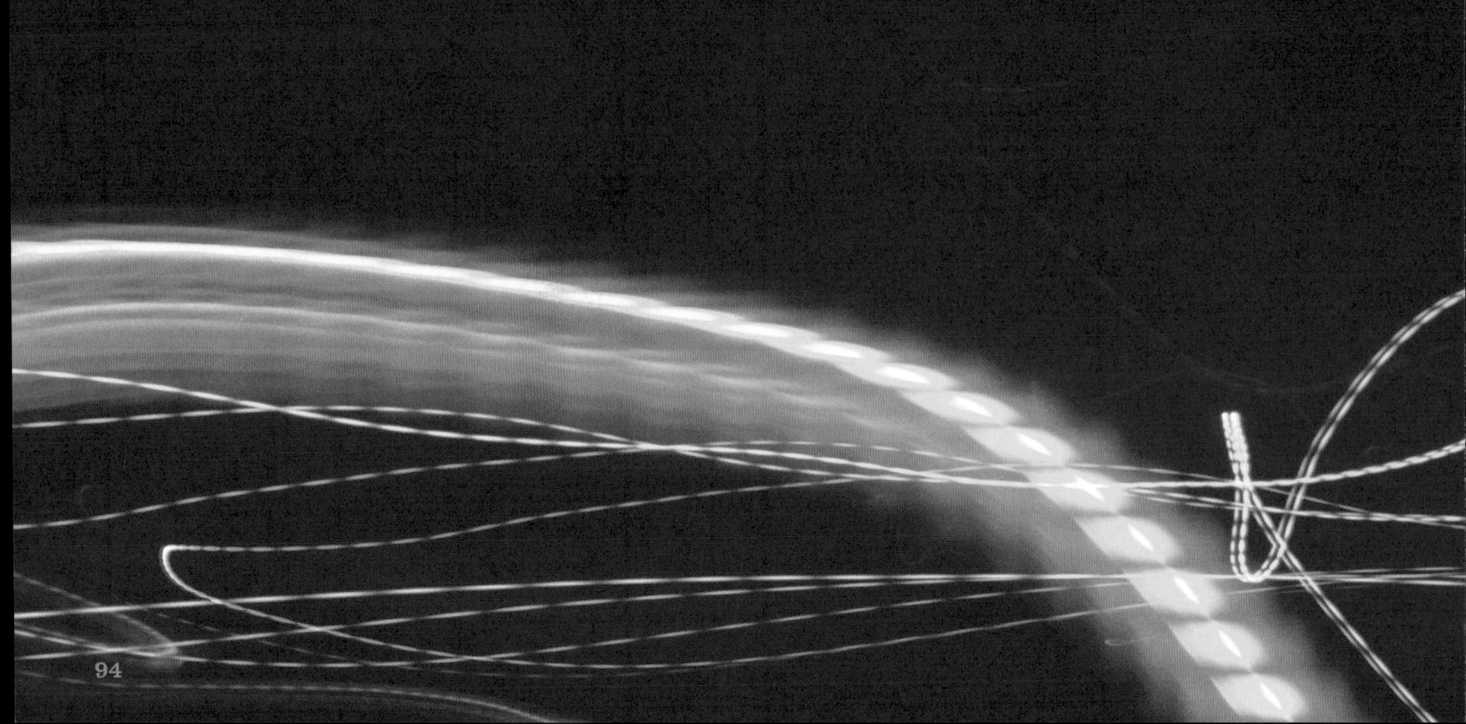

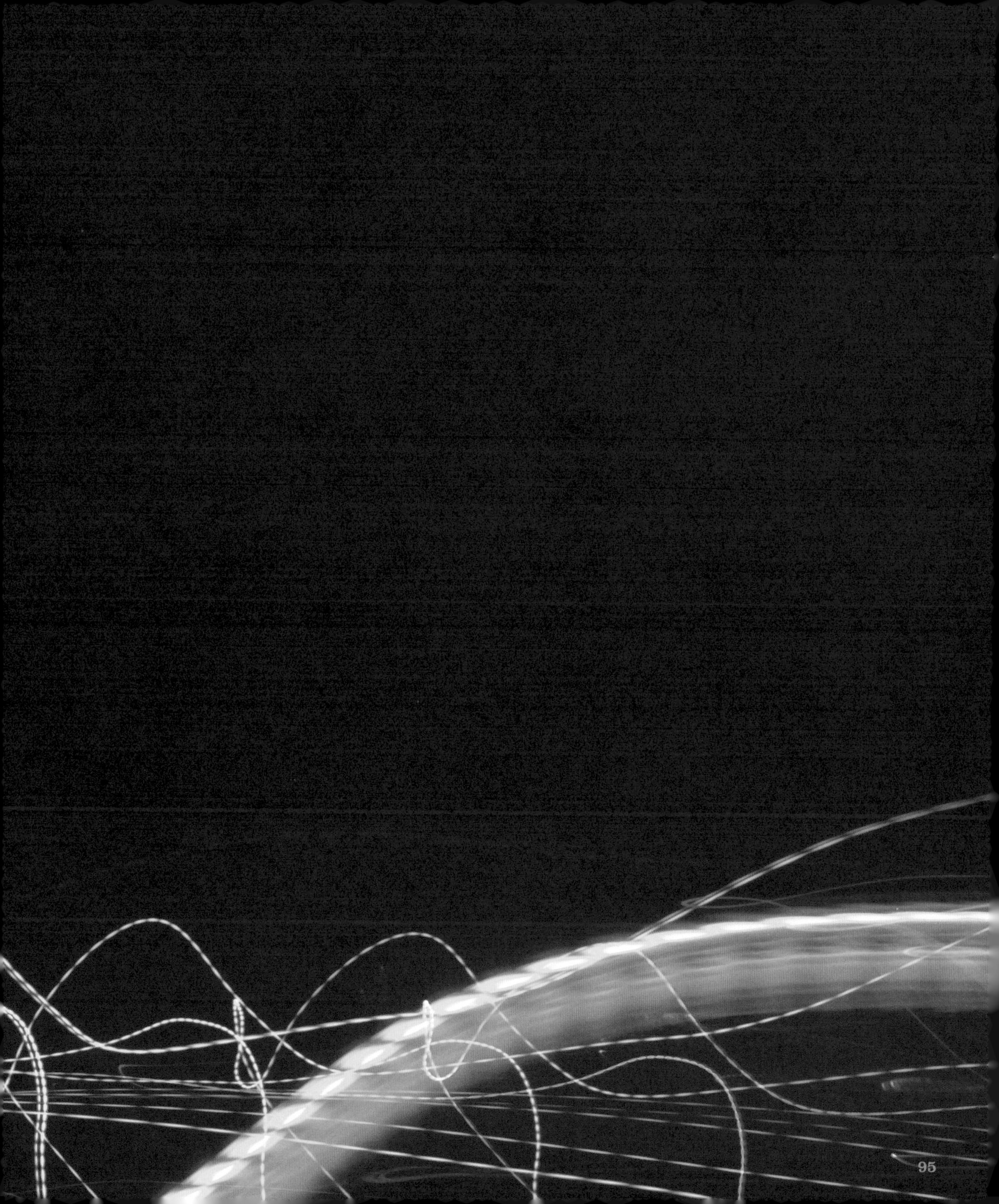

MATERIAL

When you're improvising, sometimes you'll feel like you're running out of material. It's a familiar feeling: perhaps you think you're getting boring or repetitive in your playing. Every musician has to deal with that. To solve this problem, you have to tackle it head on.

Start with listening. It always comes back to listening. Listen to one of your favourite artists, someone who you admire... Try to discover a new piece. It might be a live recording, or one from an album you haven't yet checked out. Study it, focusing in on the improvisation. Learn the solo. How does the player create variety?

Then come back to your own improvising. If you're coming from a place of ideas, then you won't run out of ideas. The way to deal with it is to try to build on your own ideas.

TRACKING MUSIC

When I listen, I automatically just start singing along. Doesn't matter where I am or who I'm with. I have a way of being able to track music I listen to and I sing a slight fraction behind, so it sounds like I actually know the solo when I'm only just learning it. The music will be playing and I'll simply try to sing along; I might miss a note or even sing phrases wrong, but it doesn't matter. It's a mixture of predicting things and understanding how it goes; and as you keep singing along, something else occurs — some kind of special magic that happens.

THE LEFT HAND AND THE RIGHT HAND

the PIANO is a
versatile instrument
which embodies multiple roles
at the same time.

left hand

There are several things that you can do with the left hand. A great place to start is playing the bassline. This is important because it spells out the harmony, delineating the sound of the chords. But you can also walk a bass, or play a groove. It's great practice learning to coordinate the two hands in counterpoint with each other. Put the time in. Start by just playing with the left hand and you'll gradually be able to put in things in the right. Make some easy exercises for yourself to help this.

right hand

Developing your right hand is a bit like developing your sense of melody. My students often ask me:

"Julian, how can I be more melodic in the way I'm soloing, rather than running scales up and down?"

My response is always:

"Well — how much melodic playing are you doing in your practice and how many scales up and down are you doing in your practice?"

left hand

Creating independence between hands is important. Start with a tune you know. If you want to loosen up the two hands, then choose a chord, try playing a simple left-hand pattern over it, then just simply play the chord. Find your way to the next chord and repeat the same process. Sometimes you'll slip up, but eventually it'll seep in and then you'll be able to play the changes using both ways.

right hand

Use your initiative. If your right hand is playing scales up and down that means that's what you're practising. It also means that that's what you're focusing on in your listening when you hear soloing. You might be thinking "I can't hear any melodic playing, so where do I get that way of playing from?" The answer is from the masters who play melodically. Check out Miles Davis, Oscar Peterson, Bud Powell, Freddie Hubbard, Wayne Shorter, Lester Young.

It doesn't have to be a pianist. You'll learn to hear like them, ingrain that into your consciousness and steal it — steal their melodies, their ideas, their phrases that work over the music that you play. Hone in on the portions of music where you run up and down scales and turn those portions into places where you play melodically. Slow it down and do it deliberately to begin with. It'll build into your vocabulary over time and that's going to help playing more melodically with your right hand.

PLAYING WITH OTHERS

Value and respect each other and
understand how you fit together as a team.

PLAYING WITH OTHERS

Playing in a group is at the core of what jazz is about — community, friendship, sharing.

Imagine you're in a group of people. Everybody's talking. Imagine you want to do something together and you open it up to the group for discussion. Your immediate reaction is that you want to make it work with this group of people. So you don't go and say, "Hey, that's rubbish, you should be doing it my way; your way isn't right." Then all you're doing is just insulting people. Music works in the same way — jazz especially. In jazz you gather a group of people who are vibing off each other, connecting with each other musically, listening to each other and trying to be empathetic and sympathetic.

Sometimes when a strong opinion needs to come in, you put it out there and then you deal with it as a group, but there are a lot of nuances to that, just like a group conversation. There's a certain democracy that we all come from an equal place; everybody's role has purpose and value, which should be respected.

Yes, we need the bassist, the pianist, the drummer, the saxophonist — whomever — you respect their parts. Then when you're improvising together that empathy becomes really important and works through democracy with mutual awareness, value and respect of each other's spaces. You understand each individual's role and how you fit together as a team — a unified musical force.

When you're accompanying, you have to take on that role and support the other musicians in your playing. Find some good voicings and rhythms that leave room for the bass and the other players in your group. It might be holding down big, sustained chords without much movement, leaving room for the bass to move around you. Or it might be holding down a certain groove, interacting in counterpoint with the other instruments and giving them some extra rhythmic energy to bounce off.

Sometimes you'll want to build your chords, putting upper structures on the top of a simple chord, but you have to experiment to get your confidence. That's where theory and understanding scales and harmony helps. Working in this way with experimentation is going to help you free up your musical vocabulary. And don't forget to listen. Identify someone whose comping sound you like and then listen more closely in order to emulate their chord building and approach so you can add to your own burgeoning language.

Just feel the mood of the group and engage with it.

IMPROVISATION

What does it mean to improvise?

Improvising is different from learning a piece of written music. When you're playing an entirely written piece, you're trying to replicate the performance perfectly from each time to the next. Your physical and mental intents have all been pre-determined.

In jazz it's not that; it absolutely isn't that.

It's more like saying that I'm going to greet you when I walk into the room. When I walk out of the room and return, you already know me. It's still me. I'm still coming into the room. That's the same. But it's different this time — I might say something different or walk in with a different manner. And that's what improvising is like. The first time is gone, and the second time is completely different — it's unique. We can acknowledge that and that's why jazz is like life. Every time you meet someone it's different, just as it is every time you improvise on a jazz tune. Jazz is the truth.

IMPROVISATION

Improvisation in jazz is being one with the moment. The ability to jump into calm or dangerous waters with excitement and anticipation to thrive. The moment is your guide, how you feel, what you want to create, how you wish to shape it, where you wish to take it and how you want to round it off. Let it flow. It could be all or none of the above — the moment is your guide.

THE JAZZ FIVE

A repertoire-driven method to learn how to play jazz better.

Learn what you love.

the jazz

INCREMENTAL SUCCESS

There are many ways we can learn music. Much of the time we're improving our technique or learning pieces that our teachers give to us. This is important to do, but it's also important to focus on what you love — the music you really enjoy listening to.

For this, I like to use an engaging five-step method I call 'The Jazz Five'.

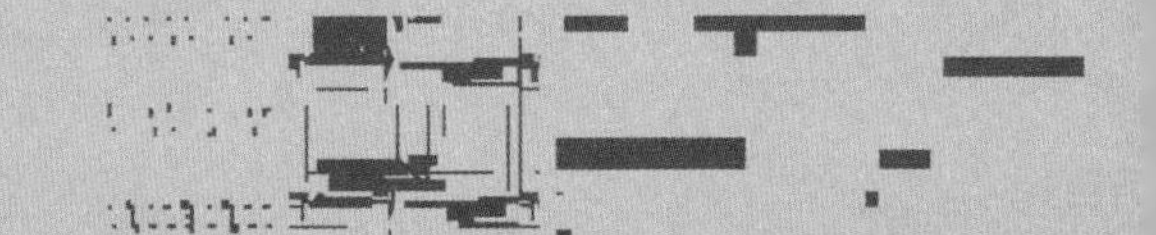

Follow this five-step process five times, each time learning a jazz standard or piece from one of the important composers from a classic period.

1.

Learn the melody from the template of a classic recording.

Really learn it, until you can perform it without any trouble.

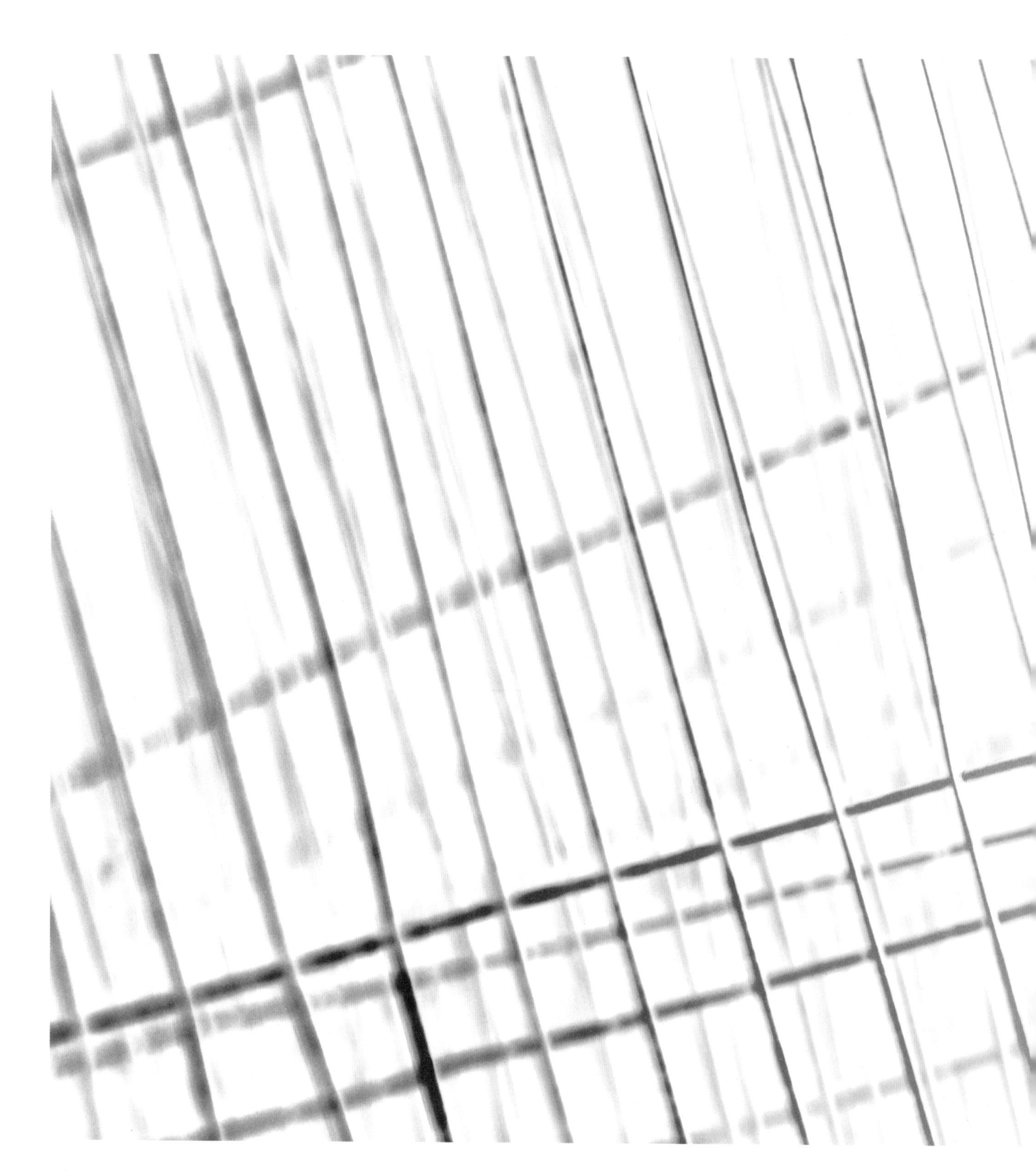

Solo over the chord changes effectively:

i. Displaying harmonic, melodic and rhythmic specificity with logic.

ii. Incorporating a good swinging feeling.

3.

Learn the root notes of the chord changes throughout the song by singing along. Do this until it becomes second nature.

Remember: the root note may not always be the same as the lowest note at any one given time on the recording.

4.

Identify the quality of each chord and sing each from the root up to the seventh, including the third and fifth.

Sing in a swingin' rhythm of 8th notes from beat 1 to the 'and' of beat 2, as this keeps you refining your swing.

5.

Sing and/or play a chorus of the solo
from the aforementioned classic recording.

Again, really learn it until you have no trouble
remembering or playing it.

5

the jazz

EXPLAINED

So what exactly is the Jazz Five?

Jazz Five is the repertoire-driven way of helping students learn to play jazz better. Students become more comfortable with learning repertoire and what to play on that repertoire. This builds a catalogue of vocabulary and sounds for use in performance and for study.

WHY FIVE?

Five is a good number. There are five fingers on each hand and being able to play five tunes has a certain satisfaction to the achievement.

Singing the different quality of the chords in particular helps you track the sound of the harmony in your ear and know what the changes are. It develops an innate sense of accuracy which doesn't rely on your instrument to really know it. It's using and developing your inner ear. Then you start to understand the bass movement as well so you're not just learning about your own role

Having the framework of the Jazz Five gives you a useful structure for learning the language of jazz. The most important part is **to try**. Learning jazz is a work-in-progress. It isn't about getting it absolutely right first time. This is why I often relate jazz to life. Most of the time when we try things out we don't get it right straight away. However, we eventually do, and this is because we give ourselves the chance. It's about allowing ourselves those incremental successes, getting better each time and never being afraid to fail. That's what the Jazz Five is.

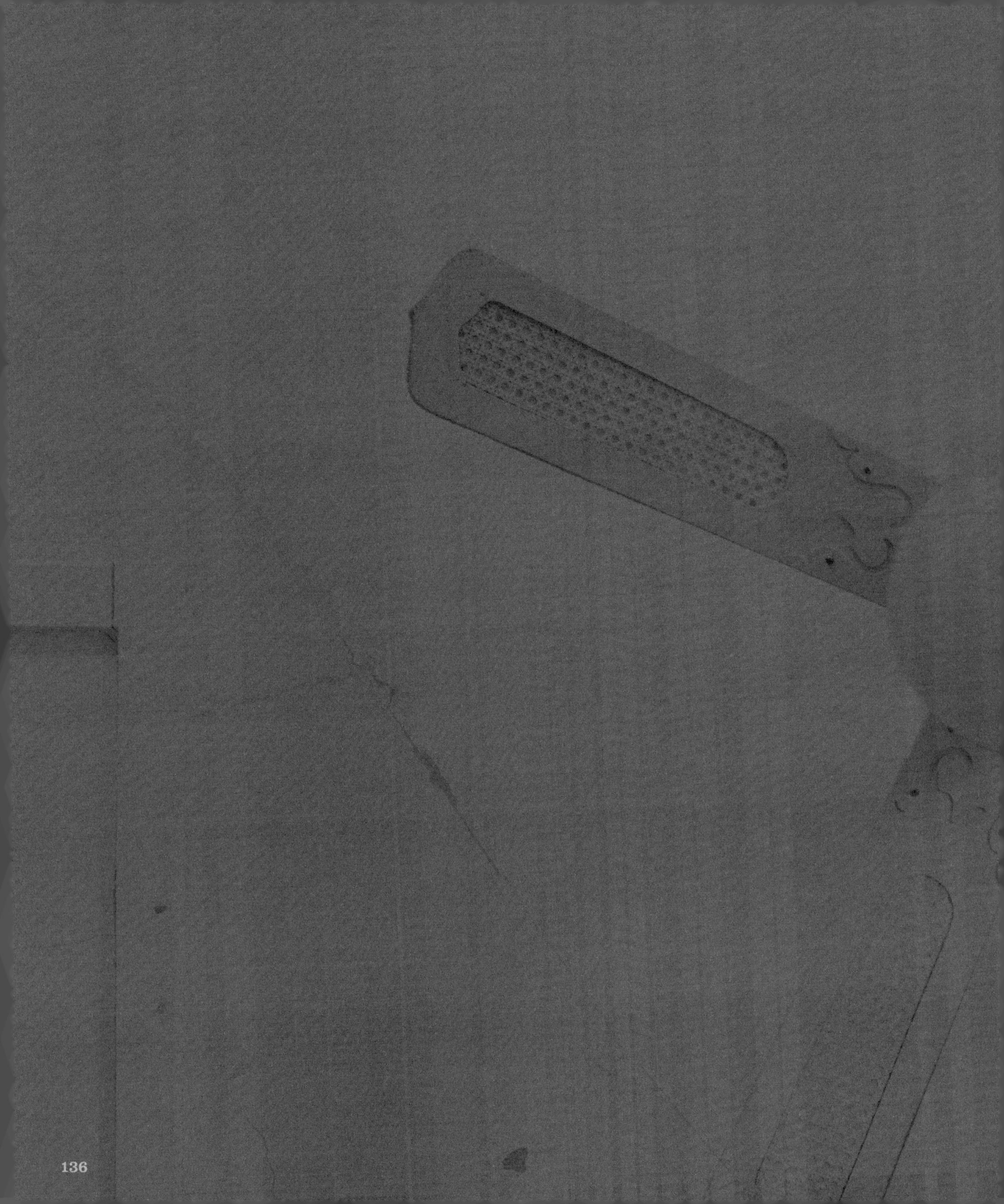

5 the jazz history

In addition to the Jazz Five, it's crucial to appreciate the roots of the music — where it all comes from. We need to look beyond the leaves to see the branch, the trunk and, with a bit of digging, the roots.

This complementary approach involves researching and understanding five historical facts associated with a particular recording.

Follow this five-step process five times, each time learning about a recording of a jazz standard or piece.

1.

Research and discover which original album or single the recording comes from, including special details like who the producer was and which record label it was released on.

2.

Find out when and where was it recorded.

3.

Research the personnel: who the players were and how they interacted, for instance who the leader of the session was and whether the group was from a well-known band.

4.

Consider and decide where the music fits in within the jazz landscape. For instance, is it swing, bebop, cool, East coast, West coast, post-bop, hard bop, free jazz, avant-garde, mainstream, contemporary, fusion... or something else?

5.

Discover an intriguing piece of information related to the tune or a player on the particular recording.

JAZZ 5 AND BEYOND

Once you have completed your first **Jazz 5** and your first **Jazz History 5**, you're on the right track. Keep going until you complete five of each.

Then what? Another five? Perhaps ten, fifteen, twenty? Sure, if you find it helpful and fulfilling. That's the beautiful thing: you can make it your own journey. Do what works for you.

I suggest living by the following laws:

1. Jazz is a music of initiative and a creative pursuit
2. Use your ears
3. Be thorough
4. Trust yourself
5. Destiny is nothing without action

When faced with difficulties:
SIMPLIFY

Listen every day and don't miss a day. If you do then make sure you catch up properly... but just because you can catch up it doesn't mean you can miss a day!

Don't be afraid to admit you don't know something, as to do so is the first step to knowing

If you can't sing it right,
how can you play it right?

Learn repertoire: working on tunes is the key to development

The key to practice is patience

Don't be afraid to challenge what's being said or played

Use your ears

Learn solos: working on solos gives insight, ideas, technique, nuance and stamina

Learn to play well (democratically and in sympathy) with others: jam, rehearse, play, enjoy

Compose: put your ideas into action and develop your own point of view

There's nothing wrong with getting it wrong at first as that's the journey you take toward getting it right! Learning is a series of failures, it is how you deal with those failures that shows your true character. Each time you fail a little less!

When practising, repeat until you "die"!

THE ORGANIC GROWTH OF ACCURACY

Jazz is many things to a great many people and I think of it as the musical language of life. As a concept it is broad, as an art form it is inclusive and all-encompassing, and as a sound it is specific with its own elemental density. Musicians in jazz are expressive, open and represented by iconic visionaries who uplift and excite us when we listen to them. Through sharing the experience of its practice we are all further nourished as players and thinkers.

In all aspects of life we grow into things — whether it be knowledge, power or a pair of shoes. It's also true that we can grow out of those same things too, until we align with what feels and ultimately is right. This progression in music and in life is what we refer to in jazz as the organic growth of accuracy.

Dream big, think big, be ambitious in your playing and your life. Create your own pathway to manage your journey toward those big dreams and you'll get there, continuing to higher levels of achievement as you revel in the joy of it all. Keep it simple, work hard, listen to the masters and you'll join the infinite continuum of jazz, exceeding all limitations. Finally, listen to yourself and use your initiative and be one with your inner jazz musician.

Thank you to my brothers John and James Joseph, with whom I started this journey in sound and continue to voraciously share music with, especially with our deep love and connection to jazz.

My niece Ava Joseph, who reflects all the knowledge that has no words, only manifestations of beauty in sound and life. My dad Howard Joseph, whose singing, playing and love of music opened my young impressionable ears. Sahana Gero, who's kindness, boundless generosity and ability to inspire with creativity is my example. My nephew Joshua Joseph who's growth and commitment to family is an inspiration. My niece Ella Joseph, auntie Joyce Wischoff, sisters Jasmine and Jane Joseph, Rev Fitz and Mrs Fay John, Cathy and Julia John and all my family and close friends imbued with the other blood — the universal blood of creation, support and existence in the continuum of life and music.

My teachers: Veronica Bradbury, Joyce Mumby, Patricia and Bert Quamby, Joan (my first significant piano teacher), Chris Johnson, Andrew Harrod, Phil Bates, Trevor Tomkins, Ian Carr, Carol Charnow, Celia Greenwood, Tom Hartman, Fred McNichol, Clifford Lee, Jennifer Bowring, Stephany Tiernan, Tom McGah, Greg Fritz, John Bavicchi, Bob Pilkington, Von Freeman, Peter King, Olaf Vas, Frank Roberts, George Coleman, Johnny Griffin and Eddie Daniels.

Mulgrew Miller, Donald Brown and Branford Marsalis three shining examples of brotherhood, friendship, commitment to jazz and what excellence and greatness in music and life looks like.

Journeying brothers, sisters and families in the continuum:

Bheki Mseleku, Cleveland, Kelly and the Watkiss family, Jean Toussaint, Steve Williamson, Courtney Pine, Mark, Michael, Valerie, Samantha, Tessa and Ethel Mondesir, Mark and Suzanne Hodgson, Seyi Sonuga, Evelyn Palmer, Tanya, Darnell, Leilani and the Miller family, Anthony Peterson, Simon and Inez Romanos, Gary Crosby, Iain Ballamy, Steve Rubie, Christine Tobin, Andy Sheppard, Jodi Goss, Adam Salkeld, Loulou Canizares, Renato Chicco, Paul Clarvis, Sonia Slany, Viktoria Mullova,

Matthew Barley and the Mullova-Barley families, Sam and Kate Walton, Geno Lenardo, Charlie Kelly, Patrick & Lella Clahar, Jason Rebello, Robert Fordjour, Dorian Ford, Carmen Lundy, Carleen Anderson, Michael Officer, Gary Officer, Des'ree, Gary Hart, Mica Paris, Michael and Nunz Csanyi-Wills, Zoe Rahman, Nikki Yeoh, Benet McLean, Sally Duncan, Amanda King, Andreas Neumann, Frank and Christian Berman, Paige Lesniak, Dan Mar-Molinero, James Gero and family, Issie Barratt, Jonathan Gee, Melanie, James and Barbara Wyllie.

Lady Helen Hamlyn, Lucy O'Rorke, Richard and Jenny Hardy, Dave Holland, John McLaughlin, Gary Husband, Steve Price, Joey Calderazzo, Ann Marie Wilkins, Kenny Kirkland, Wynton Marsalis, Victor Goines, Todd Stoll, Chad Eby, Donny McCaslin, Terence Blanchard, Donald Harrison, Reginald Veal, Bob Hurst, Charnett Moffett, Harry Connick Jr, Danilo Perez, Jacky Terrasson, Anohni, Steve Bernstein, Geri Allen, Chico Freeman, Billy Cobham, Omar, Colin Salmon, Sir Lenny Henry, Alex Pascal.

Craig Terry, Ulrich Gerhartz and all my friends at Steinway & Sons.
David Jones, Charles Bozon, Leanne Barrell and all my friends at Yamaha.

The Julian Joseph Jazz Academy family: Trevor Watkis, Byron Wallen, Tony Kofi, Alex French, Angharad Thomas-French, Tertia Sefton-Green, Adam Eisenberg, Ann-Marie Fields and the many supporting teachers, helpers, parents and students.

The incredible creative team at Music Sales, for whom this book is as much a labour of love for them as it is for me. Thank you Ann Barkway, Chris Butler, Tom Farncombe, James Welland, Ruth Keating, Polly Rockberger and Sam Lung. This book was ignited by my friendship with the wonderful Harriet Gedge, also part of the Music Sales family, the catalyst for 'Music of Initiative' and the one to whom I dedicate this book. I know she's smiling in the life eternal.

This book is also dedicated to the generosity of all the musicians who've given their time and wisdom to help shape my thinking, my students who show me that concepts and methods are always changing, growing, and refreshing from the source. To my many teachers who've imparted great knowledge and the love of sharing information, the greatest of whom is my loving mother Ursula Joseph.

Edited by Sam Lung and James Welland.
Design by Ruth Keating.
Paintings, collages and prints by Polly Rockberger.
Photography by Ruth Keating.
Lettering by Raissa Pardini.
Calligraphy courtesy of Parastou Khiaban.

Additional photography:
Pages 36–37: *Bassist Charles Mingus, drummer Roy Haynes, pianist Thelonious Monk and saxophonist Charlie Parker perform at the Open Door, New York, September 13, 1953.*
Courtesy of Bob Parent/Getty Images.
Pages 68–69: *Jazz pianist Chick Corea plays an electronic keyboard that is reflected in his glasses in this 1980, California, concert photo.*
Courtesy of George Rose/Getty Images.
Pages 94–95: *Pianist Joe Sullivan and fellow jazz musicians jamming at Ryan's, 52nd Street, New York City, November 23rd, 1941.*
Courtesy of Charles Peterson/Hulton Archive/Getty Images.
Pages: 32, 73, 78, 152 Courtesy of Fotolia.

ISBN: 978.1.78558.858.7
Order No: OP57618

Exclusive Distributors
Music Sales Ltd,
14–15 Berners Street,
London, W1T 3LJ.

Music Sales Pty Ltd,
Level 4, 30–32 Carrington Street,
Sydney NSW 2000
Australia.

Every effort has been made to trace the copyright holders of the photographs in this book but one or two were unreachable. We would be grateful if the photographers concerned would contact us.

Printed in China.

A catalogue record for this book is available from the British Library.

Visit Omnibus Press on the web at www.omnibuspress.com
Art at: www.pollyrockberger.com

As publishers, we strive to produce every book to the highest commercial standards.
This book has been carefully designed to minimise awkward page turns and to make playing from it a real pleasure.
Particular care has been given to specifying acid-free, neutral-sized paper made from pulps which have not been elemental chlorine bleached.
This pulp is from farmed sustainable forests and was produced with special regard for the environment.
Throughout, the printing and binding have been planned to ensure a sturdy, attractive publication which should give years of enjoyment.
If your copy fails to meet our high standards, please inform us and we will gladly replace it.

www.musicsales.com